KIDS AROUND THE WORLD

KIDS IN AUSTRALIA

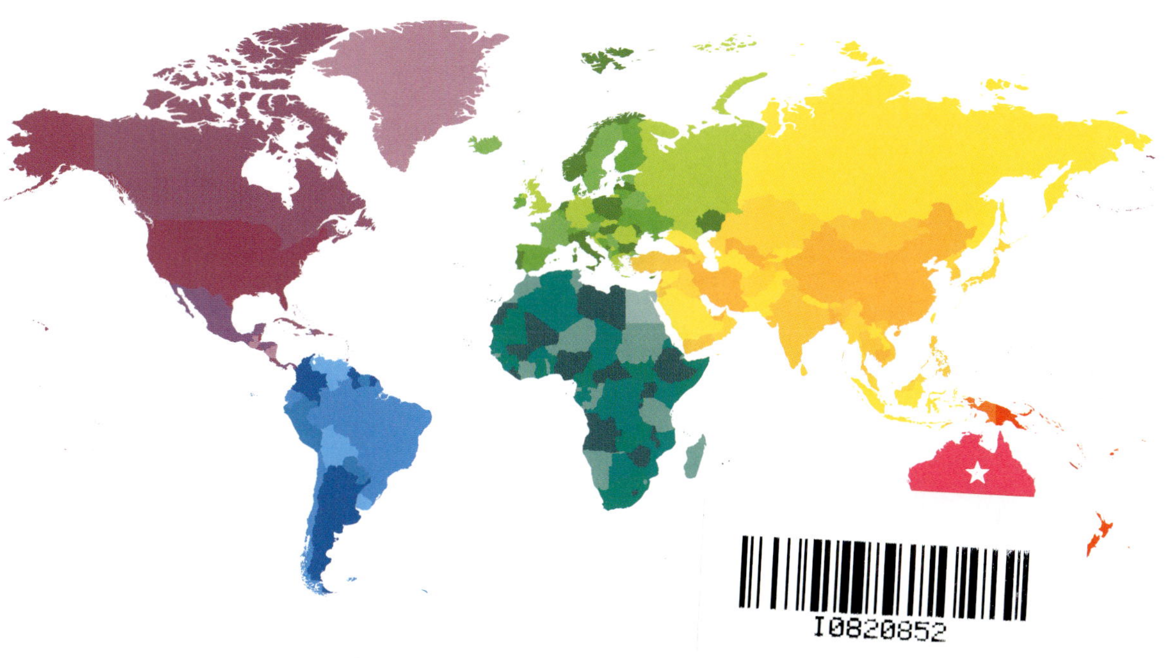

by Nikki Potts Ferguson

PEBBLE
a capstone imprint

Published by Pebble, an imprint of Capstone
1710 Roe Crest Drive, North Mankato, Minnesota 56003
capstonepub.com

Library of Congress Cataloging-in-Publication Data is available on the Library of Congress website.

ISBN: 9798875247729 (hardcover)
ISBN: 9798875247675 (paperback)
ISBN: 9798875247682 (ebook PDF)

Summary: Simple text and clear photographs describe Australia's schools, landmarks, holidays, sports, foods, transportation, and more.

Editorial Credits
Editor: Erika L. Shores; Designer: Sarah Bennett; Media Researcher: Rebekah Hubstenberger; Production Specialist: Tori Abraham

Image Credits
Getty Images: Brook Mitchell, 27, Chris Jackson, 5, courtneyk, 11, davidf, 8, 9, Izhar Khan, 28, JohnnyGreig, cover (bottom), JulieanneBirch, 7, 20, 21, Nate Hovee, 15, Paul Kane, 17, Rafael Ben-Ari, cover (top), 12, 13, Tamati Smith, 26; Shutterstock: Adam Calaitzis, 25, ChrisVanLennepPhoto, 19, Deb Rowland, 23, Elena Pochesneva, 24, Jamen Percy, 6, Jojo Textures (rainbow border), cover and throughout, la.la.land, cover (globe icon), Neale Cousland, 16, Pyty, back cover, 1, 4, Vladimir Molnar, 29

Capstone would like to thank Adrian Greaves, Melbourne, Australia, for his assistance in creating this book.

Printed and bound in Malaysia. 006460

TABLE OF CONTENTS

Words in **bold** are in the glossary.

WELCOME TO AUSTRALIA

Australia is both a country and a continent. It is sometimes called the "Land Down Under." It is in the **southern hemisphere** below many other countries.

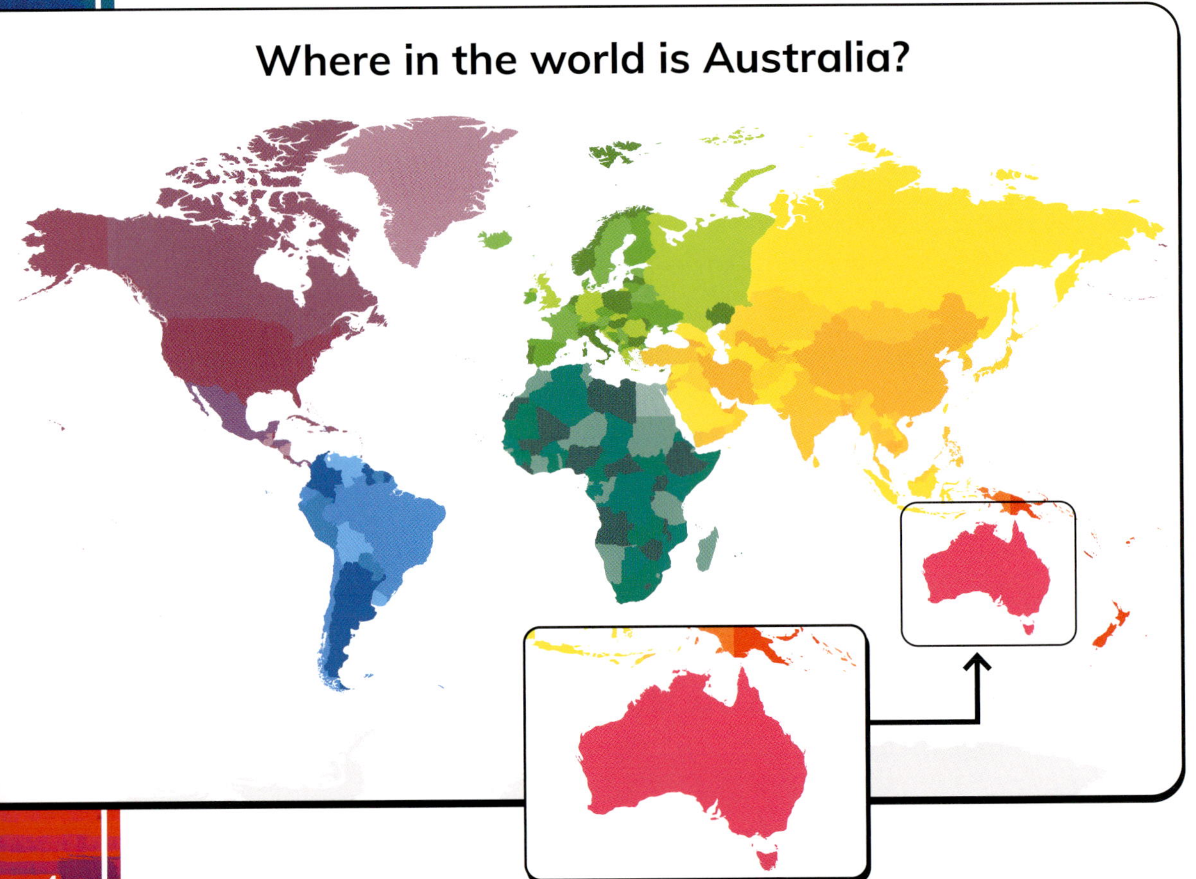

People come from all over the world to live in Australia. Most live along the southeastern coast. There are more than 10,000 beaches in Australia. Let's learn about the lives of kids in Australia.

AT HOME

Most children in Australia live in cities. A smaller number of kids live in **rural** areas. Families might live in houses, townhouses, apartments, or duplexes. Some families may have houses near the beach or coast.

Children typically live with their parents and siblings. They might have stepparents and stepsiblings. They may often see other family members such as grandparents and cousins.

TRAVEL AND SCHOOL

Some kids are driven to school by a family member. Many kids ride buses to school. Other kids might walk.

Between ages 3 and 5, kids go to preschool or kindergarten. Grades one to six are called primary school. Secondary school is grades seven through 10. Grades 11 and 12 are called senior secondary school. Kids study English, math, science, social studies, art, and health.

Australia has many types of schools. Kids might go to public or private school. Some schools are religious. The school year starts in late January and goes to mid-December.

In most schools students wear uniforms. They might wear khakis, polos, black shoes, ties, dresses, or skirts. When outdoors, kids wear hats to stay safe from the sun.

FUN AND GAMES

Hiking and camping are popular **pastimes** in Australia. Some people camp in tents. Others might stay in a cabin or camper. Families might camp along the coast. Children swim and **snorkel**. They make sandcastles.

Australia has hundreds of national parks. These are great places to camp. Kids hike around the beautiful land with their families. They see tall trees and waterfalls. They might even see kangaroos and koalas!

The Sydney Opera House is a famous landmark. There are many activities for kids there. Kids can watch plays and concerts. They might see magic shows. Kids can also participate in classes. They might make art or learn to garden.

Many kids in Australia play sports. Soccer, basketball, tennis, swimming, and cycling are popular activities.

Australian football is a top sport in Australia. It is played on an oval field. There are four goalposts on each end. Each team has 18 players.

Players can hold and run with the ball. Players can kick or hit the ball to teammates. They kick the ball through the goalposts to score points.

Cricket is another popular sport. It is played with two teams of 11 players each. One team bats. The other is in the field.

A bowler throws a ball toward a batsman. The batsman tries to hit the ball. They run across the pitch to score a point. If someone catches the ball, the batsman is out. If the bowler hits a **wicket**, the batsman is also out. After 10 outs, the teams switch.

FOOD IN AUSTRALIA

Seafood is eaten often by families in Australia. Fish, lobsters, and prawns are easy to get from the nearby ocean.

Prawns are also called shrimp.

Beef, lamb, and chicken are also eaten at many meals along with vegetables. Meat pies are popular all over Australia. These snacks are usually filled with meat, gravy, and mashed potatoes.

Fairy bread is a sweet snack in Australia. It is a piece of buttered bread. It has lots of candy sprinkles on top!

Aeroplane Jelly is another favorite treat of kids in Australia. It can be many flavors like blueberry, green apple, grape, raspberry, and more. Some might even be sour. Many people use it in desserts or just eat it plain.

fairy bread

LET'S CELEBRATE!

Australian cities have outdoor festivals all year. People listen to music, dance, and sing. There might even be a petting zoo. Kids might make crafts or watch puppet shows.

Chinese New Year is also known as Spring Festival or Lunar New Year. Families gather for special meals. They decorate homes with red paper lanterns. Families watch fireworks and dragon or lion dances.

Anzac Day is celebrated April 25. Anzacs were a group of Australian and New Zealand soldiers. In 1915, they fought a battle in Turkey during World War I. Anzac Day remembers those who fought.

Religious holidays are celebrated in Australia. Diwali is a Hindu holiday in October or November. It's also known as the Festival of Lights. Carnivals and fairs are held in large cities. December 25 is Christmas Day. People might go to the beach. It is summer in Australia.

Australia Day is January 26. Europeans first came to settle in Australia on January 26, 1788. Today, people have barbecues and watch fireworks. Some reflect on the people who first lived in Australia. Aboriginal and Torres Strait Islanders have lived in Australia for more than 60,000 years.

The "Land Down Under" is a great place to live and visit. Australia has something for people of all ages. Cricket, hiking, fairy bread, and more await in Australia!

FAST FACTS

Location: Southern hemisphere between the Pacific and Indian oceans

Capital: Canberra

Population: 26,768,598 people

Size: 2.97 million square miles (7.69 million square kilometers)

Official Language: English

Currency: Australian dollar

GLOSSARY

pastime (PASS-tym)—an activity that helps time pass in a good or happy way

rural (RUR-uhl)—having to do with the countryside

snorkel (SNOR-kuhl)—to use a tube to breathe underwater

southern hemisphere (SUH-thurn HEM-uhss-fihr)—the half of Earth's land and water surfaces that are south of the equator

wicket (WICK-it)—either of the two sets of three rods topped by two crosspieces at which the ball is bowled in cricket

READ MORE

Doeden, Matt. *Travel to Australia.* Minneapolis: Lerner, 2022.

Phillips-Bartlett, Rebecca. *Australia.* New York: Gareth Stevens, 2024.

Rustad, Martha E.H. *Animals of the Great Barrier Reef.* North Mankato, MN: Capstone, 2022.

INTERNET SITES

Australia Facts for Kids
coolkidfacts.com/australia-facts-for-kids

Australia for Kids
kids-world-travel-guide.com/australia-facts.html

Globe Trottin' Kids: Australia
globetrottinkids.com/countries/australia

INDEX

ABOUT THE AUTHOR

Nikki Potts Ferguson is a children's author and editor. Besides writing, she enjoys reading, crafting, and spending time with her family. Nikki lives in Kentucky with her husband, daughter, two cats, and dog.